Social An Disorder

The Best Solution for Your Kids for Overcoming

Shyness that Holds You Back in Your Everyday Life. (Complete Guide for Women, Men, and Teens)

David McKay

Table of Contents

Introduction

Congratulations and thank you for downloading an e-book about social anxiety

The following chapter will discuss what social anxiety means. You will get to know whether you are having social anxiety disorder or not, as well as methods to deal with it. You will know the symptoms that accompany social dysfunction and how you can analyze your social anxiety history. The book will give you the best solution to handle social anxiety.

There are several books on this topic out there, thank you once more for choosing this one!

All the effort put on this project is to make sure that you will access to complete information, please enjoy!

Why social anxiety:

Social anxiety is the feeling that will make you feel nervous, as well as uncomfortable when you are in a social setting. You may find it hard to keep it calm when you are about to meet someone new. Sometimes, you even sweat on your palms when you are about to make a presentation. Walking in a room full of strangers will make you anxious and is hard for you to handle.

Social anxiety is a mental disorder that is common in many people. Different people experience communicative complications in different ways and with contrastive stress. It is caused by an overwhelming fear that others might judge you or embarrass you. The fear that you are the center of attraction, and you might offend someone will make you anxious.

Part 1: No Worry, No Stress, How to Identify the Problem

Chapter 1: Social Anxiety and Recognizing It

What Is Social Anxiety?

Social anxiety is a normal feeling of nervousness when you are in a social situation. It is a mental as well as a health condition, but there are ways that you can deal with that. Fear will make you avoid anything that you think will interrupt your life. You will have the effects of severe stress daily when you have a social anxiety disorder. You can learn to be confident as well as how you can improve your ability to interact with people. Social anxiety can affect anyone regardless of their age and make someone self-conscious.

You tend to fear that people will evaluate you negatively, and that will make you feel inferior, and sometimes, depression is likely to hit you. You will have a problem of concentrating all your attention on yourself during any social setting. Your heart rate, as well as breathing rate, will increase, and this is a physical response that prepares you to face the situation you are about to experience. Anxiety can go to the extent of making you sleepless at nights and have fatigue. Stress does not only harm you but also has got a positive side of it. Short-term anxiety will boost the immune system

How to Recognize Social Anxiety

You cannot fail to remember when you have social anxiety or when a person close to you is dealing with social anxiety. Some signs and symptoms come along with stress in different settings. You can realize that you have fear in a social environment in the following ways;

Being Silent During Discussions

A person who has social anxiety will shy away from making their contribution during a debate. They always think that their participation will not please others or make them look ridiculous. When you have fear, and you opt to remain silent, it is a clear way to show that you have social anxiety. Avoiding an eye contact with a person is another indication that you have a concern. You will as well be unwilling to participating or sometimes, choose to stay alone instead of being with the rest in a group. When you have social anxiety, you will avoid being amongst people because you will always worry about what others think of you. You even do not have the confidence to ask for any clarification in case you need any.

Worry Because of an Upcoming Event

When you have to give a speech in a forthcoming even, and you find it hard to keep calm, it is an indication that you have anxiety. When you allow the worry to consume you, you will have side effects which include sleeplessness and digestive problems, as well as, an appetite loss. It is usual for you to be anxious in the morning of an event, but worrying about an event weeks before is a sign of social anxiety. Some people even write down the speech they are going to give, and they still feel anxious. You need to relax and feel ready for an event if you have already put down what you are going to share with people. You will, sometimes, think of changing your opinion so that you will not have to justify your thoughts. You will try at all costs avoiding the feeling of alienation as well as people questioning you. You will forge your ideas even if they are the best and you choose to go for the one another person has come up with. It can be so because you want to avoid explaining why they should go for your idea. You will feel anxious before you make your presentation, and afterwards, you may dwell on that thinking of how you made the presentation better.

Being Self-Conscious

You need to note when you are self-conscious when in a social gathering. Self-consciousness will dictate how you will interact with people. When you have social anxiety, you will be afraid of facing embarrassment as well as rejection. Extreme self-consciousness in a gathering before you get into an interaction is a way to show that you have social anxiety. When you need to talk about something that you are passionate about, and you feel that you have no content to deliver, you are likely to have an anxiety. You do not need to pay attention to your physical appearance because it will make you have social anxiety. When there are slight changes in physical appearance, you fear to appear in front of people.

Paying Attention to Fear

You will have a fear of people judging you, and you think that you will be put on the spot. The alarm can be as a result of questions that you come through from different people and in front of people. You will start panicking when fear is dominant in your thoughts.

The Feeling That You Need to Avoid Any Social Gathering

A common thing that someone will do when they have social anxiety is to avoid situations where they think they can be forced to speak. If you avoid giving a speech in front of people, you need to realize that you have an anxiety. Being nervous about how to behave when you are amongst people is an indication that you have a social anxiety. You even avoid going to places that you desire to go because you do not want to get yourself in a situation where you can address to public.

You need to know that even children have social anxiety, and you should distinguish this from shyness. It is often seen when they reach the adolescence stage, and this is when they try as much as they can to avoid social gatherings. Anxiety will make your child uncomfortable when interacting and can make them cry and even withdraw from the conversation. It can be hard for you to realize that your child has an anxiety disorder. That is why it is essential to give it a professional help when you know that your child has such an unusual behavior. As well, you need to ask whether there is bullying going on when you realize specific changes in your child.

Chapter 2: Diagnostics of Mental and Emotional Symptoms

Social anxiety symptoms are put in different categories. They include mental, moving as well as physical. Some of the ways to know that you have social anxiety are;

Expecting the Worst

Once an event is over, it is evident that you will expect people to make comments concerning the contribution you just made. But when you have an issue with social anxiety, you will not assume the best of people. You will always keep thinking about how terrible maybe you made people feel. All you feel is that you made the session boring and people did not enjoy it. Sometimes, you even create your imagination and believe that people did not find anything unusual with your presentation. You will only expect the worst from people and how they expressed the embarrassment they feel. A person with social phobia will think that they made mistakes all along, and they even wonder how they will fix errors. You will get worried about anything, and you will change nothing since the event is already gone. It is not necessary that you made mistakes, but the fear, as well as the anxiety that you have, will make you think that you are a mess. When something turns out the way you did not expect, worry comes along with concerns about embarrassment and punishment. Some people even think the worst, as though they will lose their jobs since they made a mistake unintentionally. You believe that there will be serious consequences. Some of the errors that you are likely to make may not even tamper with your content. Even when your presentation is excellent, you think that people do not appreciate the efforts you have put in.

Fear That People Will Judge You

The fear that people will judge you in the wrong way is an indication that you have social anxiety. Worrying about how people assess your appearance is the worst way to kill your confidence to be present among people. You will even end up avoiding people. You are worried that they are going to judge you on an individual basis and may not even notice what is worrying to you. They may not focus much on that and thinking that they are analyzing you will make you perform poorly. Fearing that people will judge any speech that you will give in a public place will drain you. That fear may lead to depression and avoiding places where your involvement is needed.

Fear of Embarrassment

For you to know that you have social phobia, you are always in awe that people will embarrass you anytime. You will avoid doing anything or even making a contribution so that you will not suffer humiliation. Sometimes, you don't need to say something that will trigger people to humiliate you. But you assume that when you say something, they will put you on shame. Not all the time, people are likely to embarrass you, and not all people are harmful to that extent.

Fear That You Will Be the Center of Focus

People with social anxiety fear to make a speech or even involve themselves in an activity. The reason for this is that they will attract all the attention to them. They fear that people will pay much attention to them and they might realize a mistake. They are always unwilling to make a blunder, and when one occurs, they will be in tension. A person with social anxiety will not like it when they have an eye contact with a person. They cannot keep calm when everyone is silent and listening to them making a presentation. They will avoid such instances and are never comfortable when they have to do it no matter what. When you have social anxiety, you will avoid being in charge of anything. You will prevent responsibilities because you do not want anything to go wrong, and you have no confidence to face things. When you fear trying things out, you will never make it in life.

Fear That You Look Anxious

When you are about to meet with people you are not used to, it is reasonable to be a bit apprehensive. However, anxiety can be intense to the extent that people will notice your tension. When you have a social phobia, you are likely to worry that people will know that you are not at ease. You will try your best to look beautiful, but you will not manage since you are under pressure. This anxiety can escalate to depression, and that will make it hard for you to handle. You will not want to remember that you have an upcoming event, because that will take away your inner peace. You need to compose yourself, and in that way, you will learn to take it easy. Anxiety will make you sweat, and that will make the situation even worse. When you make anticipations about the activity, you will be more anxious, and you will not be in a position to hide. The expectations that you are likely to make can even be wrong since you are already not at ease. That is how you will know that you are not ready to face people, and you have a social anxiety.

Analyzing the Entire Activity

People with social anxiety will spend some time trying to figure out as well as explaining how they made their presentation. They will start remembering the exact thing they said and trying to think where they could have gone wrong. Worrying too much about what was happening in an event after it is over is a sign that you are battling with social anxiety. It should not be the case since that means that you trust neither yourself nor the performance that you made. You need to trust yourself first so that your audience will trust you as well. When people realize that you don't have trust in yourself, they will not pay attention to you.

Fear of Being Around Unknown People

It is one of the symptoms of social anxiety. Having an intense fear when you are close to people you do not know and this is an indication that you are anxious. Being anxious will deprive you of chances to create friendships that can be of benefit to you. It will break your confidence to interact with people, and you will end up being lonely.

Difficulty in Concentrating

When you have social anxiety, you will find it hard to focus on one particular thing. If you need to prepare something for public performance, it will be difficult for you to join the dots. You will lose your concentration, and in some instances, you will find a way to miss an opportunity. You will keep postponing your deadlines to make a particular piece. Such a person will get himself finding help when it is not even necessary. On the day of the event, they will look disturbed since they are not sure whether they have the right content. In case there are other speakers before you, you will not capture anything from their presentation since you had divided attention. When you lack concentration, you are likely to miss a lot of things. Lack of focus will bring doubts in you, and that will break your confidence. Your thoughts will wander everywhere, and you are likely to end up being unable to control your obsessive thoughts. This obsession will make you feel as though you are going out of your mind. That will even lead to a total confusion.

Children who have social anxiety, express that by crying. When they have to interact with someone who is much older than them, fear will trigger them to cry. They will even refuse to speak in a social gathering and try to find refuge in their parents. Having to interact with someone they are not used to will make them panic. Some cases can be so severe and may need the intervention of a specialist. However, all is not lost, and you can recover your healthy life with the necessary approaches. You need to have a positive mindset and approach when you have to interact with people in social gatherings.

Chapter 3: Identify Any Negative Thought

Social anxiety comes with harmful and destructive thoughts. You need to be observant so that you do not hurt yourself in the process. The negative thinking is likely to rob you of the confidence that you have and feel that you cannot stand going before people. The thoughts instill fear in you, and you end up avoiding social gatherings. When you subject your opinions to negative thinking always, it will result in negative emotions. It can eventually make you feel bad and can even lead to depression. The thoughts will determine your mood for your entire day. Positive thinking will make you happy, and you will have a good feeling. Finding a way to suppress negative thoughts will be of importance to you. Replace them with positive ones so that they will not torment you. Some of the negative thoughts that come along with social anxiety are;

Thinking That People as bad

When you are in a social setting, each person tends to be busy with their issues. You can meet a calm person and befriend with if you have social skills. When you have social anxiety, you are likely to avoid people and think that people do not care about you. You may feel that you don't see your importance being there while as you are the one who is avoiding them. When you find yourself in such a case, it is time for you to know that you have to handle your social anxiety. That will make you feel like people around you do not like you and hate you for no reason.

Unnecessary Worry

It is obvious to have unnecessary worry when you have social anxiety. Even when you are on time, you are always worried that you will get late. You will portray a bad image for getting there late. In family conditions, you are worried that your partner will scold you for lateness. You do things in a hurry so that you do not get late even when you have enough time. When you have someone else to accompany you, you will make them rush. You think like they are consuming all the time and they will be your reason for being late. You will even, at times, threaten to leave them if they don't do things quicker than they are already doing.

When you need to make a presentation, you get worried about whether the audience is going to like it or not. You are not sure whether there is someone else who will do better than you. Worry will make you start thinking that your boss will not like what you have even before they make their remarks. You believe that you have nothing exciting to say. The worry will make you lose strength, and any change you feel makes you think that you are not ready. When you start experiencing such this, you need to know that you have social anxiety. You are required to have an approach that is appropriate to handle your social stress so that it will not escalate into something worse.

Judging Yourself

Judging yourself is the worst thing you will ever go, and that will make you fear. Deciding whether you will find pleasing people or not will make you have social anxiety. You will be nervous when you start thinking about how people are thinking about your physical appearance. Judging how other people will view you will make your self-esteem go down. People you are worried about will think you do not look outstanding and therefore may not have an interest in how you look but what you have to deliver. Sometimes, people do not pay attention to the minor details that are making you assess yourself unnecessarily and negatively.

Criticism

Anytime you know that you will intermingle with people, you fear they will criticize you. You do not even have a valid reason why they will criticize you, but you think it is not wise for you to join them. It is a negative thought, and you need to stop thinking in that direction. No one is going to critic you for no reason, and that should not be considered close to you. You will fear to go to social gatherings, and you will deny opportunities to learn from your fellow partners. Fearing criticism will make you an introvert, and this will make you miss those opportunities at the end. When you say something and you get someone to challenge you, it will help you be more creative. Criticism is not evil even though that people with social anxiety do not like a situation where they are subject to critics. They will avoid such situations at all cost for fear of humiliation.

Negative thoughts will only escalate worry as well as fear in you. For you to avoid negative thoughts, you can practice cognitive-behavioral therapy. That will replace your negative thoughts with those that are accurate as well as encouraging. Though it will take quite some time to replace the negative thoughts, practicing healthy thinking daily will make that natural to you. If you have social anxiety and you feel that all the approaches you use are not helpful, seek the help of a therapist. Positive thinking will help you to cope with social anxiety. When you notice that you have negative thoughts disturbing you, you should try to drop that with an immediate effect. Filter the bad and focus on the good. To change how you are thinking, the first thing you need to do is try and understand how your thinking pattern is at that moment. Do not view yourself as failure because that will never change your thinking patterns. When you avoid negative thoughts, you will be in an excellent position to fight social anxiety.

Prejudgment

Although it is wise to think about the future, the art of judging tends to be detrimental. In other words, the aspect of prejudging situations tends to be worse, especially when the opposite of the expectations is meant. In most cases, social anxiety disorder tends to cause people to decide the results of a particular situation. It is worth noting that prejudgment is done in regards to the history or rather a forecast of what might happen in the future.

In most cases, the people who are involved in this practice are always negative. Thus, they will think evil of someone and end up piling unnecessary pressure on someone. There are cases where the prejudgment causes one to overthink rather than spend quality time improving on their lives. In other words, prejudgment may force one to change all her aspects in an attempt of meeting the expectations of their peers. The peers will, in most cases, demand or look for everyday things. However, there are cases where the prejudgment predicts a near future that is yet to be accomplished. The aspect causes one to fear as they loom for an alternative as well as ways of meeting the expectations. However, when the expectations aren't satisfied, the anxiety of what the society will say pile up, and one may quickly lose his focus.

Blame Transfer

When a society or peers pile up unnecessary pressure on someone, chances of missing the mark is quite easy. In other words, one quickly loses focus and misses the point. As means of evading shame or a punishment, victims, in most cases, transfer the blame. For instance, if it issues to deal with academics, the victim may start claiming that time wasn't enough to deliberate on all issues. Others may associate their failures with the climatic changes or the lack of favorable conditions for working. There are cases where victims tend to be genuine and claim diseases as the cause of their failure. However, the art of transferring blames from one point to another tends to be detrimental and shows signs of irresponsibility.

Procrastination

One of the significant effects of social anxiety is that it causes one to fail in deliberating duties and delay them. In other words, procrastination becomes the order of the day. However, it is worth noting that with procrastination, the expectations are never met. The fear, as well as the sensation of being anxious sets in. In other words, the victim starts feeling as if they are a failure in the collective and loses focus. More time is wasted as they try to get themselves together. More fear sets in and the victim may end up being restless. Improper management of time is the primary cause of procrastination. In other words, the lack of planning causes individuals to keep working over the same issues and forget about others. For instance, scholars may spend more time with the subjects they like and forget about the others. In other words, they may end up forgetting that all the items will be examined in the long run. The sensations bring more fear.

In most cases, the realization that all the aspects will be tested in the long run causes most of the scholars to be anxious about the result. In most cases, an intense moment tends to escalate when there is no time left to deliberate on all issues. The fear of failure then deteriorates the situation. In most cases, when the scholars realize that they haven't done all of the jobs that is supposed to be done, the feeling of loss of hope and expectations of failure sets in. They start figuring about the failure they are about to experience. In other words, they start thinking of what society expects from them. The feeling of anxiety sets in, and they may not be able to deliberate on issues effectively.

Social anxiety may affect the way people lead their lives. In other words, the perception or rather the sensations that people have over someone tend to change the way one relates to society. For instance, if society expects excellence in terms of academics from you, you have to work hard to not disappoint them. In such cases, there is a sensation of fear or rather the feeling of anxiety that sets in. One starts to fear what society will judge their actions or results.

In most cases, victim becomes restless and quickly loses focus over issues at hand. They may start desiring to meet the expectations of their peers as well as the rest of society and in the long run, lose their purpose. This aspect creates some sense of irresponsibility that acts as a significant cause of failure and total loss when one is having extreme anxiety over anything.

Chapter 4: Diagnostic Physical Symptoms

The art of worrying is common to all human beings. General anxiety disorder refers to one of the most common conditions that affect individuals in the world. In most cases, individuals find themselves worrying about specific issues, but they have no control over them. The condition may get even worse so that victims may have some difficulties in relaxing or rather sleeping. The state causes some sense of confusion that might be interpreted as a mental disorder. The art of worrying is different from phobia.

In most cases, people fear specific issues that seem to be negative. However, the art of worrying is more intense and can be stressful if unattended to. For instance, people fear great heights, spiders, and snakes or rather large animals such as lions, elephants, or even leopards. Some fear thieves, and they can't walk at night whatsoever. However, the art of worrying or instead of having anxiety causes one to feel uneasy over life in general. It is often associated with feelings of dread and confusion. In other words, if you have concern about your life, you will live in a state of complications combined with the inability to relax. You may have some difficulties in deliberating over specific issues here and there. The aspect is linked to the art of confusion and the dread sensation. With the general anxiety disorder, you will be experiencing a state of constant worry, and you may not be able to avoid it. In other words, you may find out that you feel uncomfortable yet you can`t identify the cause of this constant worry. Studies have indicated that if you are in constant fear, you might be suffering from one of the mental conditions. In other words, most of the psychiatric conditions that victims experience or suffer from are related to the state of being anxious and affects the standard requirements. Victims are always confused and act to coordinate healthily.

Take a look at some of the physical symptoms that are common among victims of constant worry and stress.

Perpetual State of Constant Worry

Victims of worry and anxiety are always in constant worry. They are still having questions about what lies ahead of them. In most cases, they fear negative issues happening in their life. The art causes them to live in a state of fear that denies their ability to deliberate non-specific matters. For instance, a victim of anxiety might live in fear as though they are unable to drive or think right. They deliberately waste a lot of time when making decisions. The aspect is linked to the fact that they fear or wonder about the things that might occur in the future. The art of fear causes them to have a difficult time when choosing the side, they would fall on. In other, they are never sure of the aspect of life that favors them. They will always live in confusion, wondering whether what they have or want to will sever them well. Thus, they may even have some difficulties in making decisions over their marriage lives. In other words, the art of fear and worry causes them to lack the ability to maintain healthy and durable relationships.

Inability to Relax or enjoy Quiet Time

Anxious people will never relax. In other words, they can`t settle and may enjoy life. However, they are always fearing and wondering about their future life. The aspect causes them to lead a miserable life such that they can't enjoy a quiet time where they can reflect and deliberate on issues that might be affecting their lives as well.

In most cases, their feeling of worry causes them to keep working as they try to make ends meet. Most of them fear to lose even a single minute of their time. However, as they try to avoid wastage of time, their indecisive nature, as well as the sensation of feeling unease, causes them to keep worrying and waste more time before they make decisions. Usually, after work or after some time, people look for quiet places where they can relax and enjoy. However, anxious people will never do that. Quiet time is necessary for the sense that it allows people to relax and reflect on pending issues. It is also the right moment where one can deliberate on specific issues that affect their lives. Thus, lack of such time puts someone under pressure, and they may not be able to cope up with pending situations. Anxious people, therefore, have some difficulties in deliberating on issues. The art is linked to the fact that most of them are unable to relax and re-energize for the future — they end up piling points that create unnecessary pressure in life.

Body Aches and Muscle Tightens

Relaxation is critical for one to lead a healthy life. In other words, if you want to have a healthy life, the art of relaxing is essential. However, people who are unease can't relax. They may stay awake overnight as they deliberate and think of issues they can't control. The aspect causes intense body aches as well as muscle tightness. The minds of such individuals are always roaming, so their bodies. Most of them overwork and don't create some moments for their bodies to relax. The inability to relax causes a lot of injury to the body. The art is linked to the fact that body injuries require some time to heal. However, if one doesn't create such time, the wounds or injuries that might have been taken as one work may take time to heal. Also, the art of overworking tightens muscles and may cause general body weaknesses,which often cause pain in the entire body.

Feeling Tense

The art of worry is characterized by the sensation of feeling tense at all times. The aspect may be linked to the fact that most of these anxious people never have their tome where they can relax and enjoy life. They are always in constant fear and will never deliberate on issues effectively. They worry about everything. They keep thinking or their future growth, loss of money, the art of making profits and well as the way they can be famous. One of the aspects that causes them to be more tenses is the fact that they keep thinking of what other people will say about them. In other words, they will work hard to ensure that they maintain a good picture for the public. They are the kind of people who will eat mediocre meals but ensure that they have the best clothes ever. They are always disturbed by what other people think about them as well as their reflection on the public. They will buy expensive cars but spend their nights in horrible conditions. The tensing sensation is more of the external aspects of life that is physical. They are the kind of people who will do anything to obtain fame and authority but keep tormenting the inner person by lack of time to relax and deliberate on issues.

Avoidance of Stressful Situations

Most of these people aren't risk-takers. In other words, anxious people will always avoid stressful situations and those that will cause them to go the extra mile. They are the kind of people who will avoid duties to prevent the art of being asked questions. Most of them fear to start projects or rather, issues that might end up failing. They can`t start their own business with the fear that life will be unbearable. Their constant worry causes them to avoid issues that will cause them to overthink. It is always hard to deal with such individuals, especially where you have to share duties. Most of them will prefer taking light duties and take more time than expected to accomplish them. In other words, the desire to avoid stressful situations causes them to look for alternatives or instead responsibilities that take less time and requires less thinking. However, fear causes them to spend more time than expected. The aspect piles unnecessary pleasure in their lives, let alone others.

Difficulty in Concentrating and Maintaining Focus

Fear is the primary cause of loss of focus. In other words, anxious people can`t concentrate and deliberate issues. They will always give excuses and complain about the lack of time. The anxiety causes them to have some difficulties while thinking. In other words, when individuals lack a sense of purpose, they will always be anxious about what will happen in the future. The aspect causes them to be in constant fear such that they end up losing the necessary focus. When you have social anxiety, you will find it hard to focus on one particular thing. If you are needed to prepare something for the public, it will be difficult for you to join the dots.

In most cases, extreme fear over losing causes one to even lose more. In other words, as people are deliberating on the ways of winning over certain situations, anxious people are always thinking of the uncontrollable future. In most cases, the lack of focus and the difficulties of deliberating on issues causes them to have some problems in identifying what is best for them. In other words, they are never satisfied with anything. They will never concentrate on winning over certain situations. The art of fear causes them to multitask as they look for the ways of winning. However, the aspect increases their art of losing focus and having more difficulties in concentrating on important issues. The fear to lose causes them to lose more. In other words, when they see signs of losing over specific issues, they will be overwhelmed by fear and lose their ability to concentrate. In the long run, they lose even more.

No Tolerance of Uncertainty

In most cases, these people will always try to think of what is happening, as well as how things will end up happening. In other words, they are still anxious about the future as well as the current situation. However, their interpretation causes them to be under constant fear and end up losing. Anxiety and stressful people quickly lose their focus. The aspect is linked to the fact that they fear the art of being associated with stressful situations.

In most cases, when confronted by issues, they are fast in giving up as they are in most cases, unable to cope up with stress. In most cases, they experience tensing sensation that prevents their art of making decisions. The fear of losing and the desire to win and be great causes some sense of mixed feelings that deters them from making decisions. It is worth noting that most of these victims aren`t able to tolerate uncertainty. In other words, the fear of what will happen shortly causes them to lose over the current situation. In most cases, they act weirdly as they attempt to prevent the occurrence of negative issues. However, their art of avoiding the presence of such events worsens situations, and in the long run, more fear is instilled.

Feeling Agitated

When someone is feeling anxious, a more significant percentage of their sympathetic nervous systems goes down. In other words, there is a lot of negativity that brings some sense of danger. In most cases, when the opposite of the expectation is achieved, the victim may feel more agitated and lack the strength to keep going. Such symptoms are more intense when there are the sensations that there is an impending danger that might be roaming. The felling may also cause an influx in the rate of heartbeat, and the digestive system might also be affected. The aspect may heighten your senses, and you might find yourself overthinking. In such cases, the feeling of being agitated may be viable, especially when the fears you had come into a reality. In other words, there are cases when you are in great fear of something mischief happening. In such cases, the feeling of agitation might increase when one realizes that the misfortunes can`t be prevented. Other scholars have identified that people with anxiety aren't able to reduce arousal as quickly as people without any form of stress. In other words, they might feel agitated for long, and there are chances that they may not be in a position to control their anger. There are situations where feeling becomes intense, causing victims to experience an increased heartbeat, sweating, dry mouths as well as shaking. Such passion becomes acute when the aspect of fear is instilled.

Restlessness

Restlessness is one of the primary symptoms of being worried or instead of being anxious. Most of the victims feel uncomfortable with all situations of life. In other words, the disorder is diagnosed among teenagers as well as kids who have intense fear about their future. In most cases, the fear of what will happen shortly, as well as the sensation that one may not be able to control what is impending, makes an individual relentless and unable to settle. They are the victims who will keep speaking of a worse future and feel the lack of strength to continue instead. Such a sensation is worse as the victims may choose to committ a suicide as a means of avoiding the impending danger. It is worth noting that relentless alone may not be a good indicator that a person is suffering from anxiety, or they are in a stressful condition. However, it might be a good indication that someone is anxious or is in great fear of what will happen in the future. The victim also experiences a sensation of the unsettled mind. The aspect causes the loss of focus and the consciousness of intense fear that is not healthy. It is worth noting that the sensation of being uncomfortable and unwilling to face stressful situations causes the individual to lead a miserable life following any confrontation. In other words, when the victim of anxiety is confronted with a severe issue, the art of being uncomfortable to heighten and the individual feel more restless. There are times when the sensation becomes so intense that one feels depressed and unable to speak. Other symptoms that show one is restless is sweating as well as shaking. The victim may sweat profusely and stand still without altering even a single word. However, once the confrontation is removed or erased, victims feel themselves recovered.

Chapter 5: Reflect on Stressful Situations That Have Happened Recently or Have Been Going on for Some Time

There are various types of stress that have been affecting people in recent years. Some of these situations affect most of all individuals. In other words, location or conditions such as diseases tend to be stressful when they affect the entire nation or a community at large.

Take a look at some of the Stressful Situations

Death

No one loves or enjoys receiving the news that one of their relatives has passed or is seriously injured on the verge of extinction. The art of dying means that you won`t interact with the individual whatsoever. In most cases, the situation tends to cause a lot of changes in the functioning of the family, especially if the person who has died was the sole breadwinner of the family. It is worth noting that death remains a quagmire among families, mainly if it occurs suddenly. Such cases include accidents or calamities that aren't expected. It is worth noting that life might be unbearable if the deceased are left with no hopes. In other words, if the person who has passed on used to be the sole provider and supporter of the entire family, life becomes stressful to relatives. In other situations, people, who passed awat, leaves enormous hospital bills that must be cleared before the burial takes place. Such cases cause more harm to the feelings of individuals who are left behind. Most of them are forced to call for support from relatives and friends. Stress emerges when funds do meet the needs of the burial ceremony. The art is linked to the fact that even a coffin cost a lot of funds, and the family member might not be in an excellent position to meet such needs. It is worth noting that although death is compulsory, some sudden deaths tend to be stressful and detrimental, especially if it was least expected and the family is leaving in abject poverty.

Cancer

It is normal to fall sick and develop some illness from time to time. However, there is some condition, such as cancer that is stressful in a way. The aspect linked to the fact that their prognosis, as well as treatment, is costly and requires more resources and time. Families as well relatives might be living in object poverty. Therefore, they might not be able to offer the necessary treatment needed to curb the seriousness of the condition. It is worth noting that the treatment of cancer requires chemotherapy or rather radiotherapy that is costly in away. In other words, for one to effectively heal from disease, one has to undergo several therapies aimed at killing all the cancerous cells. There are also other cases where the person undergoing treatment fails to respond to drugs and succumbs to cancer.

The other aspect that is stressing when it comes to cancer is the situation where the disease is diagnosed at late stages. In other words, the cancer cells might have been destroying the healthy cells at a slow pace, and the victim might be living in a healthy life. However, there are cases where the condition is diagnosed when at the latter stages when drugs can't reverse the situations. The aspect becomes stressful as a lot of funds might be used, and the patient ends up dying. In other words, treatment may not be helpful, even after a lot of funds are raised.

Jobs

When one receives a call that they are employed in a particular place, there is a good feeling of joy. In most cases, people report very early in the morning as they are commencing their duties. They are jealous and work hard to please their loved ones. However, after working for some-time and getting used to the systems in a particular organization, things tend to change.

In most cases, people find themselves fighting with their bosses who gladly allowed them to work on their premises. Duties, as well as work, can be stressing, especially when one is not motivated to work more. In most cases, the rewards that one receives should be equal to or more than the work is done. However, there are no such organizations in the world. Most of the premises work for profits. Thus, they will look for ways and means of maximizing profits and reducing expenses. Therefore, they will always expect people to work more than expected. In other words, they expect their workers to work more than what they receive. Such a sensation tends to pile some pressures on workers; mainly, they are made to understand the number of profits made by such premises.

Although it is wise to work under supervision, some managers are stressful. In other words, some managers tend to be a nuisance. Most of them issue hard tasks and demand their accomplishments within no time. Most of them will fix time-tables in the favor and grant minimal permission to their subordinates. Most of them will ensure that those under their leadership work to their fullest, yet they end up carrying the day. In other words, they will be given all the praises, yet they haven't worked whatsoever. Such managers may pile unnecessary pressure on workers and demand the accountability of each step they take. The aspect denies the workers the freedom to work with minimal supervision and create some sense of humor as they work. It is worth noting that some of these issues cause one to lose the joy of working as well as the zeal to serve in particular premises. It is worth nothing that there are organizations where workers aren't paid well, but they enjoy working there. However, there are some which are well paying, but the pressure, as well as the work to be done, makes it less enjoyable. In other words, the lack of joy causes workers to lose the morale of working on certain premises. Such stressful situations are every day in the entire globe. The aspect is linked to the fact that a lot of work done by individuals is more of a mindset. In other, if one has a positive mindset, the chances are that they will be able to work well and accomplish a lot. However, dissatisfied workers are never settled. They are always in search of greener pastures. In other words, they will never set their minds on such premises. They will keep looking for places where their souls will settle and be in a good position of working. Without satisfaction, it is always hard for someone to work.

Funding Management

Money is good. It makes one drive in good cars and live a better life. In fact, without pay, one lives in a miserable life. However, it is not that people don't have money. What happens is that there are different ways in which people spend their funds. It is worth noting that money speaks. Thus, when one receives payment, the difference is created through the art of listening. In other words, those who listen to the voice in funds end up spending their funds with no limit. However, some plan for their funds and spend only what is necessary. They will never rush to do things or buy expensive items, everything in there is budgeted for. The aspect is critical in the sense that it prevents them from impulse buying and create a sense of being responsible.

However, most workers find it hard to manage their funds. The aspect is linked to the fact that most of them are paid after a month or after two weeks. In most cases, the payment finds them broke, and with a lot of expenses to meet. They are forced to pay a few bills that are necessary and left broke again. The trend keeps repeating itself for years.

In most cases, very few coins are saved. The aspect is linked to the fact that there are many expenses with very few funds. Such images can be stressful and challenging to handle. There are cases where people have committed suicide or caused a lot of havoc when few of the coins are misused. The art is linked to the fact that the aspect of looking for funds is tiresome and always tormenting.

Chapter 6: Analyze Your Personal Social Anxiety History

Over the years, the art of education and academic excellence have been the talk of the day among parents. All parents prefer a situation where their kids excel and become famous in their village. In most cases, they pile a lot of pressure on their kids so as they may work hard and pass with flying colors. The aspect has affected my parents for quite some time now. They have been pressuring us to work hard in school and excel in everything. The point of working hard comes hand in hand with a lot of costs as well as sacrifice. In other words, for one to excel in academics, there are things that one has to forgo. For instance, one has to minimize fun-time, such as watching movies as well as playing computer games. There are times where one is forced to forgo visits. However, when the results are good, one feels better and is more devoted to work harder. Parents thus prefer being associated with smart kids in terms of education. Therefore, most of them will do all that is necessary to ensure that their kids pass.

My parents have had such pressure in my life. They discovered that I could excel in academics in my lower classes when I emerged as the top student. Even my siblings couldn't believe it. However, my parents were excited and had been pushing towards my academic excellence. Although they have been supporting me whatsoever, the art of feeling anxious has been promoted. In other words, I have been concerned about the results I will get after each examination. Topping a class becomes parents have instilled more of pressure within that. Thus, I always fear losing points in any exam. It is such pressure that has been making my nerves to be awake at all time as I try to make ends meet. In other words, I have been working under pressure to achieve my personal goals and meet the expectations of my guardians.

It is worth noting that when you excel in terms of academics, society has higher expectations and always desire a situation where they will leap from your hard-work. In other words, they would prefer a position where they are proud of your achievements. The aspect means that you will always have to work hard and never fail in life. Such characters create some sense of pressure among individuals, and one feels as if it is their responsibility to work hard and lead an exemplary life. However, such situations don't happen often. In other words, there are cases where even after working hard and excelling in academics, life becomes unbearable, and one meets the opposite of the expected. Such feeling causes one to be anxious about what the society will say and think. A lot of anxiety is created, and one might end up being a failure in life. The aspect is linked to the fact that excess fear tends to be tormenting and may prevent someone from excelling in life.

The fear of what the society or rather, the community will say poses more anxiety among individuals. In other words, the desire or rather the expectation of making in life may create some sense of fear among individuals that might deter their success as well. In other words, if you are piled with unnecessary pressure, you may lose your self-identity and your focus as well. Failure worsens the situations the society doesn't expect that from you. Such kind of stress has been piled in my life. The art of passing at my lower levels changed my life immediately. The society started expecting a more excellent person in the community. Some pointed out some of the best carriers that would fit me; they would encourage me to use absolute paths so as I can amend myself. However, such expectations and pressure haven't been right in my life. The aspect is linked to the fact that one is forced to work hard and at times, meets the opposite of the expectations. Although it is good to work under pressure, too much of it tends to be destructive. It creates some sense of anxiety and restless. In other words, one is always under great fear of what will happen in the future. In most cases, the sensation causes one to over-work beyond their abilities and if things or aspects of life back-fires, one always feels depressed and unable to continue with life.

Part 2: Strategies to Overcome Anxiety

Chapter 7: Strategies to Overcome Social Anxiety

In this chapter, we are going to look at ways to overcome social anxiety. Many people today live with social anxiety and try to get over it but find it hard. Social anxiety can be avoided in very many different ways. To overcome social anxiety, people should; be confident in all they do, pay much attention to others and less to themselves, talk to trained personnel or someone they trust, attend classes and sessions that teach one how to relate well with others and with the environment, face their fears and avoid thinking negatively about their thoughts. It might be hard to try and incorporate all these ways in one's life but they are worth it since when one overcomes social anxiety a lot of changes. People who are socially anxious should do all they can to overcome social anxiety.

Anyone can be a victim of social anxiety. Men, women, and teenagers can all have the problem of social anxiety. There are times when we also experience social anxiety. One might be going to a new place where you know no one and you keep to yourself and avoid others. Whenever others are talking you are there doing your own works paying little or no attention. Social anxiety does not have to affect people who have the illness only. At times we also exhibit the disorder despite us not being victims. Social anxiety can affect both old people and young people. Men may have situations where they are experiencing the problem and women too can show characteristics of the problem. Young adults and teenagers can also possess a disorder. Social anxiety is not restricted to a particular group of people.

Social anxiety can be prevented and avoided. One should look for ways to avoid social anxiety. People exhibit social anxiety at different levels. There are some that are more intense than others and require much attention than others. To overcome social anxiety one can, identify his/her fears and look for a way to overcome them, predict the level of our fears, repeatedly do what makes you anxious and reward yourself if you manage to slowly overcome the mental disorder. The process of teaching ourselves to overcome the disorder might be hard but one should be strong and know that they are doing it for their own good. One should try as much as they can to overcome social phobia.

To overcome social phobia, one should rate his/her fears. We fear different situations in different degrees. One should rate their fears and correspondingly show to what extent they would fear the situation. One can decide to rate their fears from 0 to 10. A fear that is rated at 0 would mean that one experiences low anxiety levels or no anxiety at all when exposed to the fear. A fear rated 10 would mean that one shows high anxiety levels when the fear is exposed to the person. One should have a list of their fears because they help one to understand their anxiety more. After listing down and rating your fears, one might even come to realize they are not as anxious as they thought they were. Rating our fears helps us know ourselves better since we will know our anxiety levels of a particular fear.

A man who has social anxiety can overcome it by rating his fears. If one is a teacher and you are the master of ceremony for a certain school event and you do not know how you will do it one can rate his/her fears. One can rate starting from the lowest to the highest: addressing the school principal (4), stage fright (5), facing the students (6), being punctual and allocating time for certain speakers (7), involving the students and making them attentive and jovial (9). When one writes that down, they will realize what makes them most anxious. One comes to realize that they did not even fear to address the school principal as they expected. It is good to rate our fears so that we know who we are and where we lay.

Women too can use this method to overcome social anxiety. If you are the maid of honor in your best friend's wedding and you think there are situations that will make you anxious one can list them down. One can write: wearing the short dress (3), doing makeup (5), walking in six feet heels (6) accompanying the bride down the aisle (7), seeing people in the wedding (8), helping the bride do all that she wants to do (9). From this one realizes that tasks that require her to help the bride in all she does are the ones that make her be anxious the most. Tasks like helping the bride wipe tears when she gets emotional or helping her do something right when something goes wrong are what make her most anxious. This will help overcome social anxiety since one will know that they require a lot of confidence when doing tasks that she has rated high fears. Women too should use this method of rating their fears to overcome social phobia.

Teenagers can also rate their fears and overcome social phobia. A male teen who wants to approach a girl and does not know how to because of the fears can list them down. One can list random greetings to the girl (5), asking the girl to be your friend (6), making your stories relevant to the girl (7), and proposing to the girl (9). This helps a male teen realize whatever makes him most anxious. A female teen who wants to use this method can rate her fears too. If one wants to join a dancing club at school and is afraid that the other members will judge her since they think she is not a professional at dancing, one can list: approaching the dancing club leader (5), showing up the first time for practice (7), getting used to criticism from others (9). One realizes what makes her most anxious and knows how to deal with it. Teenagers should face their fears and rate them since they are the most vulnerable group.

One who wants to overcome social phobia should predict what will happen when faced with a certain situation. We have said above that one lists the level of their fears and by that, they will know what anxiety levels they expect. One can also predict and foretell what will happen when he faces fear. One can predict what the fear will make them do, how they will react and for what period they will remain anxious. This helps one to test how good they are at predicting things about themselves.

Sometimes we tend to react to situations better than we thought we would. Predicting and foretelling what we think will happen when faced with a certain fear helps us to overcome social anxiety.

Men who are faced with the problem of social anxiety can use prediction as a method of overcoming social phobia. In the above-mentioned situation of being the master of ceremony at a school event, one would predict that they might stammer a little when greeting the school principal, one would shake a little on stage, at times one would let a speaker take more than the allocated time and one would predict that some students might get bored and sleep or start doing other things in the background. It might however not turn out to be as they had predicted. One might not stammer when greeting the principal and find out they just feared him/her for no reason as the principal is a social person. Social anxiety victims should use prediction as a method to overcome social anxiety.

Women too can use prediction to overcome social anxiety. The maid of honor could predict that she might be uncomfortable in the short dress and she will keep on tilting it downwards for it to belong, she could predict that she will at times miss her steps and slide off a little due to the high heels, she could predict that the crowd would fix her eyes on her as the maid of honor whenever she wants to help the bride and judge her. On a wedding day, she might come to realize that things may not go as she had predicted. The dress may not be as short as she had expected and she might find many people telling her how fitting the dress is and how smart she looks in it. The crowd might applaud her for helping the bride and this will lower her anxiety levels. Predicting what we expect will happen helps us to overcome our social anxiety.

Teenagers should use prediction as a method to overcome social anxiety. The male teen can predict that the girl will not want to be his friend and she will avoid her for the first few times. He might also predict that the girl will not find anything he says relevant and he thinks that will make him lose interest in the girl and he forgets that he had an interest in her. When he tries talking to the girl, she might not be interested in the first few times but she will at one time come to accept the friendship and they create an unbreakable bond. They even become best of friends and whatever fears the boy had to get to below with time. Teenagers should not overlook predicting what they think will happen but they should use it as a method to overcome social anxiety.

People who want to overcome social anxiety should identify their safety behaviors and avoid using them. Social anxious people have ways that they think help them to lower their anxiety or hide signs of them being anxious from others. One uses behavior to cover them up. The safety behaviors should be avoided because they make one think that particular behavior is the only way you can get through a certain problem. One should find a way and stop using the behavior to cover up for them. By doing this, they will learn to do great things and have memorable experiences. One will always feel motivated to do without the behaviors that cover-up. One who wants to stop social anxiety should identify his/her safety behaviors and stop using them.

Men who use safety behavior to hide their fears should stop so as to overcome social anxiety. If a man wants to be part of a certain group of people who he thinks is cool but he is not courageous, he would think of consuming an alcohol so that he can boost his confidence. When one drinks an alcohol, most people tend to be more courageous and say things they wish they would have said long ago. He should however not take alcohol to boost his confidence so that he can approach the clique. One should do things as usual without any external effect. Asking to join the group when he is sober might be hard but once you do it you will have conquered one of your fears. Men should avoid using behaviors that hide who they really are.

Women should always be them so as to overcome social anxiety. If a woman is a chair-lady of a certain committee and she fears stating expectations of certain people, she should not use some behavior to deliver the message. She could think that not maintaining eye contact with the person at hand may make it easier to deliver the message but no. One should say and do the right thing without fear. If for example Jane has not paid the weekly contributions and that is making the group lag behind, you should mention her name and tell her straight up. It does not matter who she is or her relationship with you but you should do everything without fear or favor. Women should face their fears so as to avoid being victims of social anxiety.

Teenagers should not use behaviors that hide who they really are. If one is participating in a contest and you do not know the correct answer of a quiz yet it is your turn to answer, one may start sweating and you think of wiping the sweat secretly so that people may not know you are tensed. You should, however, let everything be. If you do not know the answer and you are at the front and everyone is waiting for you to answer then you start sweating, let everyone see you sweating. Some students might mock you but not caring about their opinions or what they think is important. How you get through the criticism is the most important part. Teenagers should not use behaviors that cover them up for their fears.

One who wants to overcome social anxiety should challenge the thoughts about anxiety. One should not always think about how anxious they will feel but overcome it. One should always be positive-minded and say to himself/herself that it will not happen like this. There are things that are negative but there is a positive side of everything we do. Being positive will help one to overcome social anxiety. One should not always keep on thinking about how bad things are or will be.

Men should positively think about their anxious thoughts. One might think in the example above that the group of people will mock you because you are not in a certain clique of people. You might think that they will not accept you because maybe you do not have the same preferences as they do. One should, however, challenge what he is thinking. One should think positively about everything. You should tell yourself that there are common things that you share. Maybe they even do not care about who you really are all they care about is your character. Maybe they even are in need of another group member. Maybe there are services that you can offer that none of them can. No one is useless. Everyone has something that they are genunely good at, that your neighbor is not good at. This is why we should always think positively. Men should not always dwell on their negative anxious thoughts.

Women also should overcome social anxiety by avoiding their negative thoughts. Onc may tend to think that in the example above Jane will hate you or influence others to hate you. The chair-lady might think that she is embarrassing Jane and that is not a good thing to do. She might think that people will start leaving the group because she is a bad leader. However, that might not be the case. The group members might acknowledge your bravery and you might be promoted to a higher level. The people need such leaders who do not fear or favor any person regardless of their status in the community. This might make the group to be known by people in society and many starts to join the group. Women should look for a way to come up with positive thoughts out of all thoughts.

Teenagers should look for a way to get rid of negative anxious thoughts. In the example, above one might be tempted to think that the other students will have a negative picture of him/her because he/she did not answer the question. One might feel embarrassed when he/she starts sweating and wonders what the rest think. One might be ashamed when the hands start to shake while holding the whiteboard marker writing on the board. One should not think in that way but tell himself/herself that the rest are just thinking about the solution to the question. That they are not even noticing that you are sweating all they are waiting for is the answer. Maybe they do not even notice your hand is shaking all they are doing is looking at their books researching the answer. Teenagers are advised not to let negative anxious thoughts overcome them.

To overcome social anxiety, one should stop putting so much attention on themselves. People tend to think that every time all eyes are on you and everyone is watching. That is not the case. People do not focus on a particular person for long. There are many people and they look at interesting things. People cannot also see our inner feelings but all they can see are our external reactions. That means that we should not let what we feel be seen externally. If one is anxious just be confident and do not let that affect how you react towards people or things. One should pay attention to what others do and not pay much attention to them. One should try to connect with others as much as possible.

Men who are socially anxious should not put so much attention on themselves. If you want to join a certain group of people but you are anxious, do not spend so much time thinking about yourself. One should not keep on thinking that people can notice that you are not fluent in talking and contributing to the stories they are talking about. One should think about others and listen to others without really dwelling on them. It is in the process that you find yourself contributing without struggling. When you create a bond with others you find everything just flows without forcing issues. Men should pay attention to others and not dwell so much on their anxious thoughts.

Socially phobic women should not dwell on them so much. In the situation of the maid of honor, one should not really dwell on you. One should not keep on thinking of the dress and how it looks on you and what people think of you, one should not think what people will say when they see you in heels or how you walk. One should put attention on others and connecting with others. People have come to witness the union not to survey people. There might be people who are judging people but one should not put so much attention on them. One should pay attention to others and socialize freely. It is through socializing that one realizes that people are not really that judgmental as one may think. Women should focus on others and not their anxious thoughts so as to overcome social anxiety.

Teenagers should not pay so much attention on themselves but in others. In the situation of the contest, the student might think that people are noticing that he/she is sweating. One should focus on what others do. There might be a student that you might look at and you abruptly remember the solution to the answer. You might look at the instructor and he/she start to explain giving you clues to the answer. One should not really put so much attention in yourself but in others. While paying attention to others, you become less anxious since for a moment you forget about the situation at hand. Teenagers should not put much attention to themselves as they put in others.

So as to overcome social anxiety, one should learn to be confident. Confidence is important because it makes people believe in you. When people realize you believe in yourself, they find a reason to believe in you. When someone does something confidently people tend to believe in you. It does not matter whether it is the right thing or not people will admire your confidence and forget whether it is right or wrong. Confidence is important as it helps one to do things believing in oneself. One might be afraid of trying something at first since it is hard but one should trust the process. Confidence is a major thing that people who want to overcome social anxiety should develop.

Men should be confident so as to overcome social anxiety. In the situation of the teacher who is a master of ceremony, if he is not confident, he will find himself experiencing all that he expected. Stage fright, stammering and bored students will be the results of a person who is not confident in his situation. If he decides to be confident, he will face the principal with so much confidence and the principal will even admire his character. He will not experience stage fright since he is confident. He will say everything believing that it is the right thing and that it will help the audience. The students will not get bored because they are enjoying listening to him. If you are confident you avoid many different embarrassing situations. A person who is not confident will keep on repeating the same thing and stammering, unlike someone who is confident. Men should strive to always be self-confident so as to get over self-anxiety.

Women who are self-anxious should enhance their self-confidence skills. In the situation of the maid of honor, one will be confident in the dress and the shoes and be comfortable in them. A confident person makes others believe in the person too. If you are confident when walking on the heels, others will oversee the confidence you exhibit rather than the small twists you make. In case you are needed by the bride and you show up confidently, people will admire you too and you will make the event a success. The bride will also be proud of you and will involve you more in what she needs you to do. When one is confident you do not get thoughts about anxiety. Women should ensure they are always confident so as to overcome social phobia.

Teenagers should always make sure that they are confident in all they do so as to overcome social anxiety. In the situation of the student at the contest, if the student is confident, he/she will not show signs of stage fright. If the student is confident, he/she will not sweat. The student will not see their hands shaking. One who is confident does not show signs of anxiety. If the student is confident, they will solve the question in the way they think is right and stand to be corrected. Schools do not only need one to be clever but also instill skills. An instructor will be impressed when they see a confident student. Teenagers should always be confident in all they do so in order to overcome social anxiety.

One who is social anxious should engage in social situations and environments. One can start attending training sessions that help one to interact with others and with the environment frccly. Once one has learned how to interact with others freely, they will no longer fear people regardless of their status and social class. It also helps one know what to say to others in case they find themselves in a situation that requires them to actively participate by talking. When one develops skills that help one to relate with others well, the people will be friendly and they will also advise the person what to do. The person also gets to meet people with the same problem or some who are already past it. They explain how they got over it and what process they went through. Attending training sessions helps one to be social and that helps one to overcome social anxiety.

Men who are victims of social anxiety should attend training sessions that help them to be social. In the situation of the man wanting to join a group of people, if he is social, he will easily fit in the group. Some people are social naturally while others find it hard to talk freely with others. The latter should attend sessions where people are taught how to interact with people. One who knows how to relate with people will exchange talks freely with the rest. He will not fear other people's thoughts because he knows how to relate to them. One knows how to deal with people who are just nuisance and knows how to deal with people who do not talk much. Men who have social anxiety problems should attend sessions that teach them how to interact with others and with the environment.

Women should attend classes if they have issues with social anxiety. In the situation of the chair-lady who wants to tell Jane that she has not paid the weekly contributions as per the regulations of the group. If the chair-lady has good social skills, she will tell Jane to pay the contributions but in a polite way. She will relate with all the group members well and they will always be happy that they have a good leader. Jane will understand that the chair-lady wants the best for the group and is not telling her to pay because of other reasons. If the chair-lady has attended the sessions she will not be afraid and she will maintain purposeful eye contact with Jane. Women should attend classes that enhance their social skills which will, in turn, help them to overcome social phobia.

Teenagers should attend sessions that teach them how to relate well with others and the environment they live in. In the first situation of the boy who wants to approach a girl but does not know how to, if he has attended the lessons, he will know how to engage the girl in talks that interest the girl. That way he will have caught the attention of the girl. He understands that the girl will not necessarily accept his proposal the first time. He will understand that the girl will not be friendly during the early stages of the friendship. He will not give up and will not show anxiety signs to the girl or the society because he has already learned that people are different and will always say something about everyone. Teenagers who are victims of social anxiety should engage actively in classes that help develop their social skills.

People who are socially anxious should find someone to talk to. One can decide to talk to a specialist or to someone they trust with their information. There are people out there who are very friendly and can help people who are socially anxious. Some people have specialized in helping people overcome anxiety.

One should try and reach out to some people. They will help someone boost their confidence and understand their fears. It might be hard to find the right person to talk to and it can also be hard when talking. At times words may fail someone but one should not give up. There are times when you expect the specialist to objectify with you but in case, he/she does not one should not give up. People should look for people who they are free with or specialists and talk to them.

Men should look for people to talk to so as to overcome social anxiety. One can look for fellow man or trained personnel. In the situation of the teacher who is a master of ceremony, he can decide to talk to a fellow teacher whom he trusts or any other person. The person may tell him that it is normal to be anxious and many people experience the same problem. He might tell him what to do and what not to do. He might be told to avoid eye contact if he thinks that maintaining an eye contact will negatively affect his concentration and time managment. He might be told to be brief in what he says and let the speakers do most of the talking. A problem shared is a problem half solved. Men should confront people they trust and talk to them about their anxiety issues.

Women should find someone to talk to so as to overcome social anxiety. In the situation of the maid of honor, the lady can find someone to talk to. If she feels anxious that people will judge her because of wearing a short dress or because she might not know how to walk majestically in heels, she should talk to someone. She might be told that the dress is not as short as she thinks it is and it actually looks good on her and so that should not bother her. She might be taught that when walking in heels you try to maintain a straight path to avoid sliding off and she might be even taught practically how to walk. Women should find someone to talk to and that will help them overcome social anxiety.

Teenagers should find someone to talk to. Teenagers find it hard to talk to someone because they do not want to be judged. You might think that someone will help you and you tell them something but instead, they end up judging you. In the situation of the student who does not know the answer to a quiz in a contest, he might consider talking to someone about the issue. The person might tell him to read and work smarter, be eager to study, ask where he does not understand and participate actively in group work. This might help him to answer questions correctly the next time he is asked a question in class. Teenagers should find someone to talk to so as to overcome social anxiety.

We should strive as much as we can to overcome social anxiety. One can try as much as he/she can and face the fears and try to understand that everyone has his/her own fears. One can list his/her fears and rate them starting from the one that makes them least anxious to the one that makes them most anxious. One can attend sessions where people are taught how to interact freely with others and with the environment. One should not put much attention on oneself and the anxiety one has but in others. You should get rid of negative anxiety thoughts. One should always be confident in whatever they are doing despite it being complicated. Social anxiety is a mental illness that we should all avoid and if we have, we should overcome. The strategies above will help one overcome social phobia.

Part 3: Mediation and Breathing Exercises for Social Anxiety Disorder

Chapter 8: Meditation

People who practice meditation are happier, healthier and in some cases prosperous than the people who do not. Practicing mindfulness and meditation has

stunning benefits to anybody who takes their time to put these skills into practice.

If in any case, you have already tried mindfulness, meditation, as well as other positive psychological interventions, you might have been for the idea that these exercises "were not for you..." after trying them out a couple of times. However, similar to any other skill, mindfulness requires practice. Do it over and over again! In some cases, the only way to achieve your goals is to find a proper direction.

Mindfulness Activities for Groups and Group Therapy

Group therapy that involves mindfulness has shown a series of reassuring results. Its effectiveness can be compared to Cognitive Behavioral Therapy (CBT) that is unarguably predominant in the world of clinical psychology.

There is also proof that carrying out group mindful meditation therapy has the same flattering results as individual cognitive-behavioral therapy (CBT). In a world with very few clinical psychologists in comparison to their need for them, as well as in a period when individual therapy time is expensive and limited, the proven effectiveness of group-based therapy is exceptional news.

You might not really feel like visiting a therapist and that is okay because there is mindfulness- focused groups that deepen and share meditation practice. Here, we will be focusing on four crucial practical exercises from such groups.

Fleming and Kocovski's Treatment Plan

Fleming band Kocovski came up with this program in 2007 as a form of group mindfulness-based treatment. It primarily aims at alleviating social anxiety. It is a good illustration of how mindfulness exercises can be integrated into a group setting because of its numerous benefits.

The treatment program entails a group of roughly 8 members who meet for 2 hours weekly for a period of 12 weeks. The first part of each session is dedicated to a brief mindful exercise followed by a discussion. The treatment program's mindfulness exercise can be broken down as follows:

Session 1: Raisin Technique

The raisin technique is unarguably the best preliminary exercise for amateurs to commence exercising mindfulness. With a variety of foods, anybody can carry out this technique. However, the exercise would be more effective if the food has a peculiar smell, taste or texture. The coordinator in this exercise gives the participants raisins and instructs them to pretend that they have never ever seen a raisin. The coordinator then brings to their attention the following things:

- How raisin feels

- How it looks

- How it smell

- How participant's skin reacts to the manipulation

- How it tastes

Directing the entire focus on raisin is aims at pulling the mind of the participant to the contemporary, to whatever has been placed before them. We may have encountered raisins almost every day but we have never taken time to really notice them

"By directing their focus on the raisin, they are holding in their hand and making an effort to notice all the details about it, the improbability of them expending time, energy and attention on ruminating or worrying about other areas of their lives."

When you systematically follow these directions and observe, it is very easy to concentrate your focus on what is before you. It is normal for your mind to wander off sometimes. All you have to do is guide it back into the exercise.

Session 2: The Body Scan

This exercises very little in terms of tools and props and it is also advantageous to beginners because it is easily accessible. For effective, somebody has to follow the following guide by the founder and expert of mindfulness-based stress reduction.

1: Here, the participants have to lie on their backs with their feet slightly falling apart and their palms facing up.

2: Here, the coordinator instructs the participants to try and stay calm during this exercise, and can only move when it is extremely mandatory to improve their position.

3: The coordinator then starts guides the body scan. This begins by participants concentrating on their breathtaking note of the rhythm and the feeling of breathing in and out. The coordinator cautions the participants against trying to alter their breathing but instead concentrate on the rhythm and feeling of breathing bin and out.

4: The coordinator shifts focus to the body: how the cloth feels like on the skin, the temperature of the body and the surroundings as well as the texture of the surface on which the body is lying.

5: The coordinator directs awareness to the sore, tingling, or feeling remarkably light or heavy, he/she instructs the participant to take note of any part of their body that does not feel anything or the parts that are highly responsive.

A normal body scan is supposed to run through all parts of the body, keenly taking note of how each area feels. Usually, the scan moves in a systematic manner through the body. For example, beginning from the feet and moving upwards to the toes, lower limbs, knees, laps, pelvic area, abdomen, chest area, upper back, lower back, the arms, neck, the head as well as the face.

After the scan is done to completion, the participants can come back into the real world by opening their eyes slowly then proceeding to a snug sitting posture.

Session 3: Mindfulness in Seeing

To some people, lacking the visual spur can result into a suffocating feeling. Ultimately, naturally experiencing a healthy imagination is not something that everybody goes through. The process of mindful seeing may be instrumental to anybody who relates to this.

It is an easy exercise that requires a window that has some sort of panorama. The coordinator instructs the participants as follows:

1: Locate a window that shows beautiful things.

2: Take a look at everything that is visible. Do not engage in any form of categorization and labeling of what you see outside the window. For instance, instead of seeing things in terms of 'stop sign' or 'bird' try to concentrate on aspects like colors, textures or patterns.

3: Take note of the movement of leave or grass in the breeze. Take note of the numerous shapes available in this miniature part of the world that you have your eyes focused on. Try to view things from the point of view of somebody who is not familiar with sights.

4: You are only allowed to observe without making any form of criticism. Stay aware but avoid being distracted.

5: In case your mind drifts away, take note of something like a color that will help revert your focus to the seeing.

Session 4: Mindfulness in Listening

This exercise is a product of the positive psychology toolkit and it presents mindfulness in listening as group therapy.

Mindfulness in listening is a very crucial mastery and can be significant to the mindfulness exercise of groups. Generally, people flourish they feel fully "seen" and "heard" and the exercise of mindful listening offers a break from directing our focus at the self or our own response.

Alternatively, mindful listening can develop an inner calmness where both individuals feel fee of judgments, preconceptions, and the listener's attention is not 'stolen' by inner chatter while grasping positive communication capabilities that are valuable.

This technique involves:

1: Instruct participants to think about something that is stressing them and something that they look forward to.

2: When everybody is done, every person shares his/her problem with the group in turns.

3: Instruct every person to direct their consciousness into what talking makes them feel, what they think about sharing with other people something that is stressful or something positive that they are looking forward to.

4: The coordinator instructs participants to observe their feelings, thoughts, as well as body reaction during listening and talking.

5: After every person gives his/her story, you then proceed to split into mini groups and answer the following questions.

a) How did it feel talking during the group exercise?

b) What did it feel like when you were listening to other people during the group exercise?

c)Was mind wandering a frequent thing?

d)If the previous answer is yes, what destructed you?

e) What did you do to bring your attention back?

f) Was your mind judgmental when listening to others?

g) If the answer is "yes", how was this feeling in your body?

h) How was the feeling like in your body just before you spoke?

i)How would you describe your feelings now?

j) What would be the outcome if you engaged in the exercise of mindfulness in listening with every individual that you engaged in a conversation with?

k) Will exercising mindfulness in listening change the manner in which you relate with other people?

l)Were there moments you felt empathic?

k) What would be the feeling if you set your focus on being attentive?

In case you need more activities to in addition to the group exercises, opt to try Qigong or gentle yoga, both of which have purposeful breath, a deliberate posture as well as the accentuation on awareness.

Mindfulness Techniques for Depression and Anger

Depression

Mindfulness is important in the treatment of depression because it reduces symptoms as well as the risk of debilitating deterioration. One study that involved eleven individuals undergoing depression came to the conclusion that there are three important aspects that make mindfulness efficacious in the treatment of depression.

I. Mindfulness assists patients in learning how to be present at the moment. This enables the patients to take some time and get hold of feelings and thoughts and as a result, choose a response that is not guided by their current emotions.

II. Mindfulness explains to patients that it is okay to give "NO" as an answer to others. This gives them a balance in their lives and also improve their confidence.

III. Mindfulness enables patients to be present with others. This means that they become more aware of their relationship and are capable of acknowledging their communication shortcomings and therefore more efficiently relate with others

IV. We have already taken a look at practices that focus on muscle relaxation and breathing. For example, the body scan and the three-minute breathing space. The Eye of the Hurricane also seeks to take a peek into your inner peace as a way of handling depression. The Eye of the Hurricane is divided into two parts. The first part introduces the Eye of the Hurricane metaphor.

When you find a place with tranquility and calmness, assume a tall but relaxed sitting posture. Inhale and exhale deeply three times, ensuring that you take it slow as you begin to feel an awareness of your body as well as any other physical feelings that may be present.

The second part is a reflection. What was the feeling like from an observatory point of view? Did you experience any other feelings during meditation?

Anger

Meditation exercises can also eject acute or chronic anger. Anger being one of the strongest emotions, it can be a little bit hard to view objectively and defuse. Mindfulness can help in creating a space between an immediate impulsive response and stimulus.

The technique below can be helpful to anyone experiencing anger:

I. To begin with, sit comfortably, close your eyes and take note of the places where your body is touching. It could be the floor, chair or mat.

II. Inhale deeply a few times to appoint that your lungs are completely filled then exhale quickly.

III. Tried to a recent time that you experienced anger. A mild type of anger is advisable in this case. Give yourself some time to experience that anger like you did the first time.

IV. Let go of any feelings that this memory brings up. For instance, guilt or sadness.

V.   Direct your attention to how you are feeling the anger in your body. Along with take note of parts of the body that are reacting to anger with sensations like cold or warmth, the impact of these reactions and whether they depict any changes when you move your body or observe them

VI.   Let go of the anger and slowly revert your attention to your breath and stay in this state for a while until your feelings have settled down or subsided.

VII. Take some time to do a reflection of the experience. Take note of the sensations that this process brought to your body. Try to figure out if they underwent many changes throughout the process. Also, figure out whether you applied anger or compassion and if so, how did you do it? Try and figure out what happened to the angry feeling when you showed it empathy.

This technique can be done over and over, as many times as it needs. It is recommended that you start off with milder anger experiences as you build-up to the most memorable and intense episodes.

Putting this technique into practice can be important in helping you defuse chronic anger in a manner that is counterintuitive: by accepting your anger issues and mindfully feeling it, you can take control of the situation and empathetically address to it.

Breathing Exercises

Breathing exercises is an excellent, fast and easy solution for anxiety and stress relief. Proper implication of breathing techniques works on anxiety issues at a psychological level by naturally slowing the heart rate. The effects of anxiety are almost instantaneous. Considering the fact that relaxed breathing is a psychological plan, this approach is almost universally efficacious for getting relief from anxiety. It is almost impossible to go wrong with it.

Before you get started, keep the following tips in mind:

- Do not force it. This can intensify the stress.

- Think of a suitable place to do your breathing exercise This might be your bed, your bedroom floor or on a comfortable chair.

- Put on comfortable outfits.

Super Simple Meditation Breathing.

Breathing exercises do not have to be complicated. Super simple meditation breathing is a simple breathing exercise that is arguably the most successful anxiety relief technique. The main trick behind it is to breathe slowly. You need to completely ignore how you breath in and focus on how you breathe out. The length of your breath will increase naturally when you breath out for a longer time. That is why there is no need to consciously focus on how you breathe in.

When you are breathing out, try and make it slow, gentle and steady. Some people liken this process of blowing a balloon, slow, steady and with a very little amount of force. Breath out entirely until the last drop of breath is let out.

As you breathe slowly, also try to take note of places in your body that may be holding tension. Usually, these places may include your shoulders, lips, and jaws. Every time you breathe out, try to let out the tension as well, and let relaxation to come in.

Deep Breathing or Slow Breathing?

People usually think that it is advisable to use deep breathing techniques for anxiety relief. However, putting your focus on a slow kind of breathing is much easier. Breathing slowly is less likely to generate deep breathing anxiety that comes about when people take a deep breath.

Breathing slowly is one of the best breathing exercises for panic attacks because it helps you in slowing down your heart rate and consequently naturally causing a calming effect on all the body systems involved in your body's flight/fight/freeze response. This is because the slow breathing exercise discussed above is simple, it is not easy to fail to remember the instructions when you are battling panic attacks.

A Slightly More Involved Breathing Exercise

If you would like to get to know a myriad of meditation breathing exercises, you have to consider attempting alternate nostril breathing. This is equally an easy, natural breathing exercise for managing stress and anxiety. This technique can be performed by closing one nostril by gently placing your finger on it. Breath out then breath in through the open nostril. After every complete breath cycle, change the nostril that is being covered.

Breath Focus.

While you engage in deep breathing, create a picture in your mind and a phrase or word that will boost your relaxation. You can do this as follows:

Close your eyes, breath in a few deep breaths. As you breathe in, imagine that the air has a sense of tranquility and calm. Make an attempt to feel this way throughout your body. Breath out, and as you do so, imagine that the air going out is taking away the tension and stress. This time around as you breathe in again, say to yourself in silence, " I breathe in calm and peace." When breathing out, say to yourself, " I am breathing out tension and stress. "Repeat this procedure for 10-20 minutes.

Equal Time for Breathing in and Out

This technique involves matching the duration of your breath-in with how long you take to breathe out. As you keep doing this over and over you will notice that you are capable of breathing in and out at a time.

This technique can be practically executed as follows:

Ensure that you are comfortable sitting on the floor or a chair, breath in and as you do so, count to five, breath out and count to five as well. Repeat the same process a couple of times.

Progressive Muscle Relaxation

This exercise involves you breathing and simultaneously tensing a muscle group and consequently releasing the muscle group when you breathe out. Progressive muscle relaxation can be very instrumental in case you want to have a sense of physical and mental relaxation.

This technique can be carried out as follows:

Lie comfortably on a flat surface, breath in a couple of times to relax, breath in again and this time tense the muscles of your feet almost simultaneously

, breathe out and let go of the tension on the muscles, breath in again and this time tense your calf muscles and then breath out and let go of the tension in the calves. Do this over and over as you work your way from your feet to your head and tense the muscles in every part of the body.

Modified Lion's Breath

As you carry out this technique, assume that you are a lion, open your mouth wide and let out all the air.

This technique can be practically executed as follows:

Ensure that you sit either on the floor or on a chair, breathe in deeply to ensure that you fill your belly with air, when you can no longer breath in any longer, open your mouth as wide as possible and let out the air with an '?"aaaah..." sound. Repeat the same procedure several times.

Simple Abdominal Breathing Exercise for Relaxation

The next time you are stressed or anxious, try this simple but effective relaxation exercise:

Breath in deeply and slowly through the nose. Make sure your shoulders are in a relaxed position. Ensure that your abdomen balloons and that your chest rise is minimal.

Slowly, exhale letting the air out through your mouth. In the process of blowing the air out, purse your lips a little bit and ensure that your jaw is relaxed. Normally, you will hear a "whooshing" sound as you exhale. Repeat this process for several minutes.

This breathing technique is very convenient because it can be performed as often as needed. You can do it will be standing up or lying down.

If you find it hard to do this exercise, or you feel like it is making you panic or more anxious, suspend it for some time. People with panic disorder sometimes feel an increase in panic and anxiety whenever they do this exercise. This may be a result of anxiety that is brought about when you focus on your breathing or simply because you have not practiced the exercised hence you are not doing it correctly.

Building Confidence Skills

Unlike a set of rules, confidence is not something that can be learned. Confidence is a state of mind. Thinking positively, practicing, knowledge, training and engaging in meaningful conversations with other people are some of the ways to boost or increase your confidence.

Confidence emanates from feelings of physical well-being, accepting your mind and body(self-esteem) and believing in your skills, expertise, and ability. Confidence is undoubtedly an attribute that almost everybody would want to possess.

There are two sides to revamping confidence. In as much as the primary goal is to feel unruffled, it is also crucial to take into considerations how you can make other people see you as a confident individual. Below is a list of ideas of how you can achieve this.

Planning and Preparation

Normally, people usually feel less confident about unfamiliar or possibly tough situations. Perhaps the most predominant way to develop and maintain confidence is by preparing for any uncertainties.

For example, if you are applying for a job, it would be wise to prepare for the interview. This involves planned what you would want to say as well as brainstorming some of the questions that the interviewers may ask you. Practice your presentations for the interview by doing mock presentations to your friends and letting them give you feedback.

Another crucial aspect of the interview that will either make or destroy your confidence is grooming. Make an attempt to visit the hairdresser and also work on the outfit you will wear on the day of the interview.

Ensure that you are in control of uncertainties the best way you can. The best way to do this could be by breaking down major takes into sub-tasks and handling every issue extensively.

In some instances, there might be a need for you to have contingency plans. These are back up plans that come to your aid when your main plan backfires. For instance, if you had planned to use your car to go for the interview in the morning and the car breaks down midway, what would you do? Being able to react calmly to such kinds of uncertainties is a sign of confidence.

Positive Thoughts

A positive thought can be a very formidable way of boosting your confidence. If you have the belief that you can achieve certain goals, then you are most likely going to channel your energy and hard work to make sure you do. However, if you doubt your ability to reach certain goals, then chances are that you will face the challenge halfheartedly and there the chances of you losing are very high. The only solution is convincing yourself that you have what it takes to do something. You just need the right support, knowledge, and preparedness.

In addition, there is also a load of information about positive thinking on the internet as well as in print. This kind of information will help you take note of your success and strengths and consequently help you learn from your mistakes and weaknesses. This is much easier than it sounds. Usually, we often over concentrate on mistakes that we made in the past consequently ballooning them into bigger issues than they were in real sense. These kinds of negative thoughts can be hazardous to your confidence and consequently your ability to achieve your goals.

Try to recondition the way you think

1. *Know Your Strengths and Weaknesses*

In this case, the best way forward would be to come up with a list of the things you are good at as well as things that need to be revamped. So as to ensure that the list is not biased, use the help of your family, friends and close associates to help you come up with the list because they are the people who know you better. After coming up with the list, highlight and congratulate yourself for your strengths and work on improving your weaknesses.

2. We All Make Mistakes

Do not perceive your wrongdoings as setbacks but rather as learning opportunities.

3. Use Criticism as a Learning Experience

Everybody sees the world from different angles, and what always works for one person may not work for another. Critics are just people giving their opinion. Be confident when being criticized and do not reply in a defensive or aggressive manner or let your self-esteem wounded by criticism.

4. Talking to Others and Following Their Lead

Finding Yourself as a Role Model

Normally, this would be somebody that you see from time-t-time, perhaps a fellow worker, a friend, a family member. It must be someone who is very confident and who you would like to emulate. Always take time to take a look at and note positive traits categorize them as confident people. How do they talk? what posture do they portray when they walk around? what do they say? how do they say it and when do they say it? How do they react when they make a mistake or are faced with a problem? How do they socialize with other people? and how do those people react to them?

If it is possible, take time to talk to them so that you can get lessons on how they go about their business and what makes them stand out?

Being surrounded or talking to people who are confident normally helps you to feel more or less like them. Take lessons from people who are often efficient in accomplishing their goals and tasks that you wish to surpass-let their confidence be a motivator factor.

As you build your confidence, more and more, offer advice and help to other people who are in the same place you were some time back. Take up the role of being a role model for somebody who has confidence problems.

Experience

When we efficiently accomplish tasks and reach our set goals, the confidence that we can similar and even tougher tasks increases. The best example, in this case, is driving a vehicle. People who have been driving for a while do not overthink what to do and how to do it. They automatically know what to do, whether it is on a sharp bend, a stop sign or even a junction. This is the direct opposite of a learner driver who is mostly engulfed in nervousness and has to be extra cautious with how he/she handles things in the vehicle. The learner driver does not have the experience hence their unsteady confidence in their capability to drive.

The process of gaining experience, more so taking a leap of faith to make the first step can be extremely difficult. Usually, the thought of coming up with something new is usually scary than doing it. This is where learning, preparation, and positive thinking come in handy.

Breaks tasks and roles down into small goals that are achievable. In addition, ensure that your goals match required criteria. They should be specific, measurable, attainable, realistic and timed.

In whatever you take part in, aim at becoming the best that you can. This is because the better you are at doing something, the more confident you become.

Be Assertive

Assertiveness basically means defending what you believe in as well as sticking to your integrity and uprightness.

Being assertive can also mean that you are flexible enough to change your mind if think that it is the right action to take and not because you are being pushed to do so.

Confidence, assertiveness, and self-esteem are closely interwoven. In many cases, people start portraying assertiveness when their confidence develops.

Keep Calm

There is usually a close relationship between calmness and confidence. If you feel calm about tackling an important or difficult issue, then you are confident. Whenever your confidence sublimes, you more likely to depict nervousness and stress.

Being calm regardless of whether you are under stress and pressure tends to give you a feeling of confidence. To achieve this, it is crucial to teach yourself how to relax even intense situations. Research and learn any relaxation technique that works best for you so that you can put it into use whenever you are stressed or under pressure. This might be as easy taking a couple of deep breaths to slow down your heart rate and consequently bring you back to a state of normalcy.

Smile and Look People in the Eye

This idea sounds so obvious but the truth is that when you put on a smile, you feel cheerful and more confident. Nonetheless, very many people despise the power of a smile in their everyday lives.

When you make eye contact and then crown it with a smile, it depicts a sense of warmth and easiness in you. This gives the people you are interacting with the reassurance that you are approachable and sociable, thus tweaking the quality of your interactions. Once you start interacting more and in a better way with other people, your self-confidence improves to a point where you can communicate naturally.

Greeting people with gentle eye contact and a warm sincere smile shows people that you can be trusted. That you intend to engage in an entirely peaceful conversation hence you are not a threat to them. This is a show of assertiveness and which is beneficial to both parties in the long run and helps build confidence in both individuals as well.

A great percentage of people who do not have self-confidence are afraid to keep in touch and connect with other people. They are willing to do so but because of the fear of rejection, they opt not to. People rarely approach them they do not smile or make eye contact hence they send the wrong message to other people. A genuine smile with gentle eye contact can be open doors to great opportunities.

Avoid Arrogance

The more confident you become, the more accomplished you become. Therefore, any form of degradation on other people should be kept arm's length. You should keep in mind that nobody is a perfect being and there are always new things to learn every day. Give a compliment to whoever deserves it but make sure that it is sincere. Practice and use politeness, courteousness and get involved in what other people are doing by asking them questions and engaging in discussions.

Part 4: Dietary and Exercises

Chapter 9: Diet and Exercise to Overcome Social Anxiety

Tips About Social Anxiety and Diet

The long-known truth is that there is a chain of chemical reaction that is present when a person is eating and the food is getting digested. These foods and the chemical reactions have the influence of determining how a human being feels. It is important for a person to be mindful of the type of food he or she is taking for the sake of feeling hungry. The foods that a person is supposed to really check on them are the fast foods that are fallen for after busy days at the fast-food joints.

The forms of advertisements that are being promoted have been switching peoples' attitudes. The new waves of advertisements are targeted at creating awareness of the foods being advertised. They have tried to incorporate the essence of letting the consumers know of the health benefits those foods have on a person's body. The process of advertisements can also lead to a person being anxious. It is because there are specific foods that are being pushed for specific people which triggers too much pressure on some people. There is no need for a person to worry since there are several tips, he or she can use to control his or her diet. They include:

1. Linking Exercise to Diet And One Can Beat Social Anxiety

Exercise has been proven to having several benefits. The vigorous process has been successful in helping people who are affected by social anxiety. The process can be described as a reliable practice that improves a person's concentration, reduces fatigue and improves the general cognitive function of a human being. There have been several studies that have been able to show that exercise that is vigorous and continuous has the ability to reduce depression levels for up to 25% in an individual's life. By linking, diet and exercises will help a person to boost his or her mind.

2. Being Aware Of The Link That Is Between Anxiety And Eating Disorders

There have been several types of research that have been conducted on the relationship between social anxiety and eating disorders. This is despite the lack of direct form that interlinks the two phenomena that one can lead to the other. However, it will be beneficial for a person just to be armed with this kind of knowledge. What people do not know is that appearance anxiety and fear triggered by fear of negative evaluation and have the potential to provide a person with vulnerabilities in two interlinking factors that are disordering eating and social anxiety.

3. Watch What You Drink

There are several triggers that can be mirrored by a person's body as physical symptoms for social anxiety. Drinks such as alcohol have the ability to prevent a person from dealing with social anxiety. The available knowledge is that alcohol can be used to unmask several feelings such as when a person is not comfortable. Despite these advantages, this drink does not provide healthy solutions for a person seeking to cope with social anxiety.

4. Not Getting Dehydrated

Do you know that little forms of dehydration have the potential of triggering anxiety in human beings? This case is severe in females compared to the other gender of males across the global village. There is a part of the brain which is responsible for triggering thirst. It in turns triggers the drive of a person to finding water. The process of finding water has the potential of making a person feeling worried which can be perceived as a trigger of social anxiety.

5. Minding Of The Caffeine Intake

This can be another contribution from dehydration. Caffeine also has a greater influence in mimicking an individual's body responses that are witnessed when a person is in a mental state of fear. The common factors that are prone to be observed include twitchy muscles and a racing heart. These two displayed occurrences have the potential of triggering anxiety in an individual's heart.

1. Watching Out For Food

There are several things that are inculcated at this point. An individual can look at how he or she reacts to dairy products. He or she can go ahead and look at the response he or she gets from foods such as cakes, pasta or even sugary drinks. Several people have certain types of food that make them feel a little odd making them switch moods. This might be a cause of anxiety in an individual's life. Therefore, a person is supposed to be mindful of what he or she takes in because it is not about just the chemical reaction. It is good for an individual to know which kinds of foods that can be able to bypass his or her food sensitivities.

2. Restarting The Day In A Hearty Way

The life we leave in is filled with several activities in the morning. There are people who are supposed to take their kids to schools, there are people who try to rush to their workplaces and there are people who try to rush to schools. These activities make a person be in haste of having breakfast-making them not to have good meals in the morning. This forms a poor start for the day because of the types and combinations of food that they have taken. A person is advised to have breakfast that is highly pretentious because it gives an individual good and a swift way of releasing excessive energy. It makes the body to avoid going through a rough patch before it is allowed to consume lunch.

3. *Eating Complex Carbs And Beating The Sugar Rush*

There is a certain way that an individual's body breaks carbohydrates. The body takes a much longer time to breakdown whole carbohydrates compared to sugars and processed carbohydrates. This means that foods that have high sugar content have the potential of giving a person a sugar rush. This might lead to a person experiencing the rush in energy making a person have an insulin rush. It leads to the rapid fall of the insulin levels in an individual's body leaving him or her feeling low or down.

4. *Knowing Of One's Vitamins And Minerals*

A smorgasbord of detailed information is out here in the global village about several foods. The most focused on foods are those with high levels of vitamin B, omega-3s and magnesium. These stated foods nutrients play a very important role in a person's happiness because they are interlinked with an individual's mood. One is able to access more information from a nutritionist. This is because a person is able to control his or her mood by knowing what he or she is consuming. It also gives a person the power to control what he or she is consuming in his day to day life by having the knowledge of the chemical reaction process that involves drinking and eating.

5. *Not Falling For Fat Diets*

It is very important for a person to be very mindful about what he or she is consuming. One does not have to wait for the moments he or she has to eat many lemons or end up eating nothing throughout the day. A person has the power of regulating anxiety in his or her hands. It is because he or she can be able to regulate what he or she consumes throughout the day. This does not have to mean that a person has to create a regulatory diet for him or herself.

Exercises That Can Help an Individual Overcome Anxiety

There are several moments that an individual can experience anxiety in his or her life. During these moments, there are several exercises that an individual can choose to undertake. These exercises have the ability to calm an individual who is stressed out in his or her life. The goals of these exercises are to help an individual to relax in moments he or she is stressed out. They include;

Relaxing by Breathing

There are several things that an individual can be able to notice when he or she is anxious. The most common occurrence is the increase in the palpitation of the heart and the rate of breathing also increases. A person can begin to sweat or begin to feel light-headed and start sweating. During the situation of feeling anxious, an individual is supposed to be able to keep his/her breathing under control. This has the potential of making an individual's body to relax.

There are several steps that an individual can use to get his or her breathing under control. The first step involves an individual finding a good spot that is comfortable and quiet and seat. Place one of his or her hand on the chest, the other hand is supposed to be placed at the stomach. One's stomach is supposed to move more rapidly when the person is breathing. The next step involves a person taking regular breaks slowly through his or her nose. The process is done as a person watches his or her hands from where they are placed. The hand placed at the chest is supposed to remain still while the one which is placed at the stomach is supposed to have slight movements. The third step involves a person breathing slowly through his or her mouth and doing it slowly. The process in entirety is supposed to be done for a span of ten minutes until the levels of anxiety lessen.

Relaxing by Visualizing

A person is supposed to be able to find his or her happy place. It might seem to be like a difficult or undoable task. However, it is a simple task that involves a person being able to paint a perfect picture in his or her mind. The perfect picture painted is about a beautiful place than has the potential to calm an individual's body and his or her brain.

When a person begins to feel anxious, he or she is supposed to find a place that is comfortable for him or her. The place is supposed to be clear of any form of sound distraction because it is supposed to be a place filled with silence. The next step involves a person thinking of an ideal place he or she can relax. The place can be anywhere across the world even places he or she has never traveled to or just an imaginary place. Despite all these, the place a person is settling for in his or her mind is supposed to be a place where he or she feels calm, peaceful and safe. An individual is supposed to be able to return to this place when he or she is feeling anxious at any point in life.

Thinking of the finest details about the places created in the mind is the task a person is given. These finer details entail how is the smell of the place or envision how the place is supposed to smell. A person is supposed to be able to know how the place feels and the sounds present in the place. Then a person is supposed to envision him or herself in that perfect environment enjoying the serenity of it.

Once a person has the perfect envisioning of the place, he or she is supposed to close his or her eyes and take regular breaths. These breaths are supposed to taken in through the nose and taken out through the mouth. An individual is supposed to be aware of his or her breathing while at the same time focusing at the perfect place he or she has envisioned. The process is supposed to go on until the levels of anxiety in a person are relieved or calmed down. Once the process is successful, a person is encouraged to regularly visit these places in moments he or she feels anxious. It is because the success of calming down has a high chance of reoccurring.

Relaxing Of One's Muscles

Moments an individual feels anxious to make the body have a shift from its normality. A person is able to notice the shift of muscles to them being tensed or a strain in the muscles. The occurrence has the potential of making the life of an individual difficult. It is because muscle stress can make an individual have a difficult time when he or she is managing anxiety in moments he or she is experiencing. If a person is able to release the stress levels in his or her muscles, then he or she can have absolute power of reducing the anxiety levels in his or her life.

There is always a quick way an individual can use to relieve or reduce the anxiety levels. The process involves a person using five steps for it to be successful. The first step requires a person to look for a place to sit and relax that is comfortable and free from noise. A person is supposed to close his or her eyes after he or she is settled and then focus on his or her breathing. One is advised to breathe slowly and swiftly. Oxygen intake is supposed to be done through the nose and exhalation done through the mouth.

The second step involves a person using his or her hand. He or she is supposed to clench a fist and squeeze the fist to his or her tightest of his or her ability. The third step requires a person to hold on to the clenched fist for a while. The estimated time for this step is a couple of seconds. An individual will start realizing all the tension he was feeling in his or her muscles is been channeled to the fist. The fourth step is about a person opening the fingers in a slow manner and realizing how he or she feels. It is easy to notice the tension leaving the hand as the fingers are being opened. The last part of the process entails an individual continuously releasing after tensing various groups of muscles in the body. These muscles group of muscles include those in the hand, feet, shoulder or legs. It is great if the process is done from the muscles that are down a person's body going up. However, an individual is warned from tensing muscle areas with injuries because of the pain it can inflict on a person's body.

Relax by Counting

Counting is one of the easiest ways an individual can use so as to reduce anxiety levels. This method is widely known and practiced across the globe. When a person feels that he or she is anxious, he or she is supposed to identify a place that he or she feels that it is safe, comfortable and silent. He or she can close his or her eyes after sitting down and try counting from one to ten. If this process proves to be necessary to an individual, he or she can go ahead to counting up to twenty. The technique is not limited because an individual can go to a higher number of his or her jurisdiction. The counting act is supposed to be done continuously until a person feels that the anxiety levels in him or she have subsidized.

There are moments that the relief is able to occur quickly. There are certain moments that the process can take a while for its results to be witnessed. Therefore, a person is supposed to be able to stay calm and patient throughout the process. Counting helps a person to relax because it makes an individual focus on a different thing rather than the anxiety itself. The process can be used in an unfavorable environment without silence. These environments involve crowded places such as stores, trains or even public gatherings.

Relaxing by Staying Present

This practice is referred to as mindfulness. It entails a person being able to be present by noticing one's current state and his or her surroundings. It goes a notch higher by requiring an individual not to be judgmental about his or her surroundings.

The process has its own benefit to a person practicing it. It helps him or her finds a calm state. This is advantageous when he or she is anxious or his or her thoughts are racing.

How does one achieve this state is the major inquiry. There are several simple steps that an individual can use to gain this state in his or her life. It involves a person finding a quiet place that is comfortable and then closing his or her eyes. The next step will require a person noticing how he or she breaths and how his or her body feels at that current moment. An individual is supposed to switch what he or she feels to the environment around when he achieved to know the state of his or her body and breathing. This entails feeling the environment, noticing the smell of it and the sound that is emanating from the place. The process is supposed to do back and forth on the body and environment until anxiety fades.

Relaxing By Interrupting One's Conscious Thinking

It is very hard for a person to be able to think in moments he or she is anxious. The kinds of thoughts prone to emanating at this point are very dangerous. It is because these thoughts can be untrue sometimes and have the potential of making a person do certain things that can escalate the levels of anxiety. Therefore, it is very important for an individual to break his or her thoughts during these moments when faced with anxiety.

There are several ways an individual can be able to break his or her thoughts. These ways include;

- An individual singing a song to a different tempo or speaking out one's anxiety issues in a funny and different tone

- Choosing a nice thought to focus on rather than focusing on such as a person thinking of his or her loved ones or lover

- Listening to music or reading a novel or book

Chapter 10: How Exercises Help to Fight Anxiety

There are several benefits that exercising brings to an individual's life. The potential fighting diseases and improved levels of a person's physical condition are some of the benefits that have been established for a very long time. Physicians have been among the spreading awareness of encouraging people to stay physically active.

Exercising has been found in helping an individual to stay mentally fit. It has the potential of helping an individual reducing his or her stress levels. There are several studies and research that have been done on other benefits of exercising. They have been able to release that exercising helps a person to improve a person's alertness and level of concentration. The process helps a person reduce his or her fatigue that with the day to day activities an individual does in his or her daily life. The cognitive functioning of the brain is helped by exercise. There are several times that stress has the potential to deplete a person's energy.

Stress affects the brain first before the impact is felt by the rest of the body. The numerous nerve connections in the brain then transfer the impact to the rest of an individual's body. On the other hand, a person's body is predicted to feel better in moments his or her mind is in a good condition. There is a certain hormone that is produced when an individual engages him or herself to several exercises or other forms of physical activity. The hormone produced is known as the endorphin hormone. The hormone serves several purposes in an individual's life that are very beneficial. Endorphin is responsible for relieving the pain that one experiences during the day to day activities. The hormone helps to improve the quality of sleep a person gets. The two stated advantages of endorphin help in the reduction of anxiety levels in an individual life.

Scientists have invested quit of their extensive search on regular participation of aerobics to the mental state of a person. The study has been able to reveal that exercise helps to reduce the levels of tension in an individual's life. This has several impacts in return that help in calming of anxiety. It improves a person's self-esteem, stabilizes his or her mood and improves his or her sleep. People are encouraged to participate in exercises for at least five to ten minutes every day. The process has the potential to give out anti-anxiety effects.

It is normal for an individual to experience stress and anxiety in his day to day life. Therefore, it is important for one to choose a perfect form of exercise he or she likes. It can be dancing, weight lifting or jogging. During these sessions, an individual's heart palpitations tend to rise as the heart palpitations. The phenomenon helps a person's heart to function even better than earlier on. This brings about the result of resting heart rate becoming slow during the exercise sessions. When a person has an improved functioning of the heart and lungs, he or she is associated with having an overall great sense of general well-being. This is very important when a person is offsetting the feelings of anxiety.

Studies even go ahead to showing that exercises have the ability to prevent anxiety attacks from happening. A recent study depicted that when a person does regular exercises, he or she has the potential of reducing anxiety attacks by 25%. This advantage has the potential of lasting for five years if the exercises are done continuously. The chemicals that are produced during these exercises give a person the fortitude to focus through anxiety attacks because they can kill emotional pain during those moments.

There are several ways that an individual can be able to make these exercises to be effective. The first form has been depicted which includes choosing an exercise that one finds enjoyable. These physical activities are supposed to have achievable targets. An individual is encouraged to take simple runs for ten minutes than waiting for a marathon done after a week or month. The most important thing is that the exercise is done frequently. A person can add something different during conducting his or her exercise such as listening to music. Therefore, one can carry a portable media player such as phones or iPods for this purpose. Recruiting someone to do these exercises helps to break the monotony and improve one's level of commitment in the process. The last advice given to a person is being able to remain patient because results from this process would not be instant but gradual.

There are several climatic changes that are witnessed day in day out. There are several things that an individual is supposed to know when he or she is exercising in cold weather. He or she is supposed to be able to dress in layers. These pieces of clothes can be removed when a person begins to sweat. An individual is supposed to protect his or her hands and ears by wearing gloves and headbands. During the sessions, one is supposed to pay attention to the environment and head into the wind.

Chapter 11: 30 Minutes of Exercise a Day Would Be Sufficient

One of the most recommended ways that help in dealing with anxiety is exercising. This is common advice that people who have faced anxiety and stress have been given by several people. However, it becomes a difficult task for a person to identify which type of exercise is fit for the purpose. It is important for a person to know which exercises can be effective to achieve the goals set for the exercise. An individual is not supposed to be worried about there being only one form of exercise. The good news is that the exercises that can help break anxiety and stress are several. This means that a person has a variety of options to choose from.

There are three major exercises that stand out over the years. They are effective because they are a combination of several activities in them. The issue of anxiety is supposed to be taken with keen interest because it affects several people across the globe. Statistical research by the Anxiety and Depression Association of America found out that around forty million of the adult population in the United States of America ails from an anxiety disorder. A third of the total forty million are the only ones that tend to seek treatment and help for anxiety. Therefore, the rest of the people are advised to at least do exercises whether at the gym or an open field. However, an individual is warned about having a bad perception that exercise has the potential of healing completely anxiety attacks. If an individual feels more overwhelmed during any of this exercise is supposed to seek professional help.

The exercises that are encouraged in this chapter have been scientifically backed to have a positive impact on anxiety. The exercises are supposed to be done for an amounting time of thirty minutes for an individual to gain optimum benefit from them. These exercises are favorable to anybody who is either a beginner in exercising or someone who is used to exercising. These exercises include;

1. Aerobic, Cardio-Heavy Exercises

These types of exercise are majorly known for pushing an individual's heart rate to go up. Some people describe them as busters of anxiety in the psychology field. This form of exercise includes several exercises that are widely practiced by people across the globe. The process includes exercises that have high intensity such as running, team sports, swimming, and weight lifting. These exercises have the ability to make someone breaking a sweat, increate an individual's heart palpitations and hard forms of breathing.

A good explanation of this process can be drawn from the study conducted by Harvard Health. They have the potential of reducing the stress hormone in an individual's body. The most common stress hormones are cortisol and adrenaline. They help the body to produce a special kind of hormone that kills pain in an individual's body which is known as endorphin. This hormone also helps a person to have elevated moods during the day while active. Endorphin hormone aids human beings to find forms of relaxation and be optimistic which are resulted from intense moments of working out. After these exercises are over, an individual is supposed to have warm showers.

Aerobic exercises have heightened success when it comes to dealing with anxiety. There are several studies that have been conducted on aerobics by several scientists. A study conducted on people ailing from anxiety found out that their symptoms dipped for ninety minutes after an intense exercise of thirty minutes. The workout had a person have a maximum oxygen intake of eighty percent which made breathing become very hard. The massive amounts of energy an individual puts on aerobics help to lower the levels of stress hormones and improve the levels of endorphin hormone.

2. Intense Work Outs

An interesting study done in the year 2010 found that intense work out to up to thirty minutes has myriad benefits to an individual. A session of work out can be accompanied by several exercises that are beneficial to an individual in reducing the levels of anxiety. The results are optimum if an individual is able to push him or herself to doing vigorous exercise for thirty minutes and not less than. The interesting finding of the study was that it was easy and less anxious if the activity is done for a period of three months and not a lifetime.

There was an intriguing reason that was behind the stated point above. The basic thought by the researchers was that continuous exercise was responsible for increased palpitation and the breathing of an individual. These were things that helped a person have a comfortable feeling and helped a person when he or she was ailing from anxiety. It is because the symptoms of anxiety are characterized by an increased form of breathing and racing of an individual's heart.

The thirty-minute dedicated by a person to this exercise is supposed to be able to help him or her to maintain low levels of anxiety. It is because the signs and symptoms of anxiety reduce overtime when the process is continuous. The intense workouts are supposed to break into three parts for it to be sustainable and efficient to beginners. The intermittent breaks are supposed to be after ten minutes accompanied by a five-minute rest.

3. Yoga

This is one of the ancient practices developed by human beings. Yoga practices have the potential of lowering the levels of anxiety in an individual's life. It is because the technique has the appearance of modulating the response systems that are responsible for stress management. The practice of yoga has the potential of reducing the levels of psychological arousals. There are several forms of psychological arousals which include respiration, heart rates, and blood pressure. The act of yoga centers its advantages on two key pillars which are its ability to calm an individual and the physical strength it gives him or her.

Intense sessions of yoga which are done up to thirty minutes have the potential of calming an individual. This is because it reduces the stress and it improves the palpitation of an individual's heart. The process helps the brain of a person to relieve from racing thoughts since it is shifted to focus on a person's breathing and the gentle and fluid movements. One of the common symptoms of anxiety is a person having low levels of continuous worrying and being too vigilant. These are some of the anxiety symptoms that yoga constantly alienates in an individual's life. These stated benefits of yoga were proven on three people in the year 2016. The research was conducted by Georgia State University which found yoga decreases general worrying in a person's day to day life.

Chapter 12: Several Pieces of Evidence Suggest That the Exercises Are Really Helpful

The first form of exercise that its evidence can be illustrated is those from yoga. Several techniques that help in the reduction of anxiety levels have been developed from the years of the 1970s. The exercise of yoga has seen several interests from people in the modern world despite being in existence for a long time. There are several pieces of evidence that have been used to support the rise of this practice. A good depiction can be found in the United States of America. The statistics available show that nearly 7.5% of the adults in the American population have been able to try out yoga exercise. The findings go a notch higher to showing that nearly 4% of the adult population practiced yoga in the past year.

The evidence of yoga being successful is traced by the rise in the number of people who are practicing it. The process modulates the systems in an individual's body that is responsible for stress control. A good depiction was done by the University of Utah. The study was looking at the impact of yoga on its participants in response to pain. The study had a total of forty-two participants. There were twelve participants who were experienced at the practice, sixteen healthy participants and fourteen participants who have issues concerning stress.

The three groups of people were subjected to both low and high levels of pain. The group of people with stress-related issues was able to feel pain when it was exerted at lower levels. This was different from the rest of the two groups of participants. The research was able to show that people who felt so much pain had several activities that were being processed by the brain. The research was able to show that people who practiced yoga felt pain when it was inflicted in high pressure. The group of yoga practitioners had low pain-related activities in their brains. The research on the brain was able to be conducted by the use of MRI machines.

There are several pieces of evidence that have depicted the importance of exercising in an individual's life. Randomized research that had forty trials which were randomized was conducted on three thousand patients. The research revealed that the group of patients who held constant exercises had a twenty percent reduction in their anxiety levels. This was compared to the rest of the patients that participated in the exercise. Exercises such as cycling, walking, and weightlifting have reported major success across the globe which has made them be prescribed by psychiatrists in their therapy sessions. The randomized clinical trials that were conducted had the potential of giving individuals accurate information from the data collected. This is because the process used is described as golden standards for clinical research. The patients used in this research were ailing from different health conditions. This included patients ailing from cancer, arthritis and heart diseases. There were certain conditions that were focused on by the researchers which included feelings of nervousness, worry, and anxiety in a person.

Chapter 13: Benefits of Exercising on Anxiety

There are several people who think that exercising is all about muscle size and aerobic capacity of a person. The thinking angle is straight since exercising can help a person to trim his or her waist, add years to a person's life and improve one's physical life. However, these factors cannot be described as elements to help a person to stay active in his or her day to day life.

There is another motive to exercise. This motive is that exercising has the potential of making a person have high levels of well-being and self-aware. The process of exercising helps a person who does it constantly to have enough energy that can get him or her throughout the day. The practice goes ahead to make an individual have better sleep when he or she rests after finishing his or her daily activities. The other advantage exercising brings to an individual is it improves his or her memory and make people have positive feelings about themselves. This makes them have a relaxed form of life that is very important for a person when he or she wants to achieve his or her goals. One is supposed to realize that exercise has various importance in an individual's mental health

The benefits exercises bring to an individual's brain come after a long span of days. The process can take an individual thirty to sixty days for the results to be depicted. A person is then advised to be very patient while he or she is exercising out. The call of being patient goes in hand with an individual being consistent with the type of exercise he or she is doing until the results start popping out. The results from these exercises are very advantageous because they relieve stress; promote the quality of sleep and improve of an individual's mood. Researchers have shown an individual does not have to a workaholic on exercising since a modest amount of exercise can produce required results.

Exercising is a natural way that is effective in aiding to cure anxiety. The first step the process does is that it relieves tension and reduces stress levels in an individuals' life. It goes not higher in boosting a person's mental and physical energy. The process of exercising helps to control anxiety by producing an endorphin hormone that is responsible for the well-being of human beings. It is great for an individual to put his focus on things that keep him or her moving. It will be a waste if a person zones out while this process is ongoing. There are several ways that an individual can keep and maintain his or her focus while exercising. A person can choose to count his or her steps while walking; he or she can decide to concentrate on the sensations that are produced when he or she is running such as the rhythm being produced or he or she can choose to focus on the flow of wind. This will definitely improve one's awareness in turn.

CPSIA information can be obtained
at www.ICGtesting.com
Printed in the USA
BVHW091420160221

600149BV00005BA/158